SAP Certified Application Associate - SAP S/4HANA Cloud, public edition - Manufacturing

by

Pete Smith

Copyright Notice

Before you Start..

Before you start here are some Key features of the **SAP Certified Application Associate - SAP S/4HANA Cloud, public edition - Manufacturing** certification test.

This certificate is the ideal starting point for a professional career as a Manufacturing consultant on SAP S/4 HANA.

This certificate proves that the candidate has the required understanding within this consultant profile, and can implement this knowledge practically in projects under guidance of an experienced consultant.

✓ Associate Certifications are targeting profiles with 1 - 3 years of knowledge and experience. The primary source of knowledge and skills is based on the corresponding training material.

✓ The exam is Computer based and you have three Hours to answer 80 Questions.

✓ The Questions are (mostly) multiple choice type and there is NO penalty for an incorrect answer.

✓ Some of the Questions have more than one correct answer. You must get ALL the options correct for you to be awarded points.

✓ For questions with a single answer, the answers will have a button next to them. You will be able to select only one button.

✓ For questions with multiple answers, the answers will have a 'tick box' next to them. This allows you to select multiple answers.

✓ You are not allowed to use any reference materials during the certification test (no access to online documentation or to any SAP system).

✓ The Official Pass percentage is 62%. (This can vary slightly for your exam)

Questions with Answers

Question: 1

Imagine you are a business owner who wants to streamline your organization's processes and improve efficiency. You have decided to implement SAP Central Business Configuration to achieve this goal. Which of the following capabilities will you have access to through this solution?
Note: There are 2 correct answers to this question

A. Provisioning the quality and production system
B. Deploying the solution scope
C. Maintaining Business Users
D. Migrating data

Explanation:

As a business owner who wants to streamline your organization's processes, SAP Central Business Configuration provides you with two key capabilities.

First, you can provision the quality and production system by creating and setting up the required systems, including development, quality, and production environments. This ensures that your solution runs smoothly and efficiently across all stages of the development lifecycle.

Second, you can deploy the solution scope by defining and configuring the business processes and functionality that your organization requires. You can activate and deactivate features, manage configuration settings, and adjust the system behavior to meet your specific needs. This is crucial to ensure that your organization is using the SAP solution in a way that optimizes efficiency and effectiveness.

Answer: A, B

Question: 2

In the SAP standard scenario SAP EWM Integration - Outbound Processing to Customer (2VK), which of the following activities is carried out in the SAP EWM system?
Note: There are 2 correct answers to this question.

A. Post Goods Issue
B. Create Delivery
C. Assign Worker
D. Replicate Delivery

Explanation:

In the standard scenario SAP EWM Integration - Outbound Processing to Customer (2VK), there are two activities that are carried out in the SAP EWM system. These activities are:

- Post Goods Issue: This involves confirming that the goods have been shipped to the customer. In this process, SAP EWM sends the information to SAP ERP regarding the goods to be shipped, and once the delivery is created and all necessary checks are completed, SAP EWM sends the confirmation back to SAP ERP that the goods have been shipped to the customer.

- Assign Worker: This activity involves assigning a worker to a specific task, such as picking, packing, or loading. In SAP EWM, the work order is created, and then a worker is assigned to the task based on their skills and availability using the work centre.

It is important to note that other activities, such as creating a delivery and replicating a delivery are typically carried out in the SAP ERP system.

Answer: A, C

Question: 3

Which business role is used to perform the process step "Record Inspection Results" in the SAP Best Practice Quality Management in Warehousing (3M0)?

A. Warehouse Operative
B. Quality Technician
C. Quality Engineer
D. Warehouse Clerk

Explanation:

The business role used to perform the process step "Record Inspection Results" in the SAP Best Practice Quality Management in Warehousing (3M0) scenario is the Quality Technician role.

The Quality technician role is responsible for performing quality inspections and recording the results in the system. In the context of the SAP Best Practice Quality management in warehousing (3M0) scenario, this role is responsible for recording inspection results in SAP EWM.
When a quality inspection is performed on a product, the Quality Technician performs the necessary checks and records the results in SAP EWM. The system then updates the inspection lot status and the stock status accordingly.

Answer: B

Question: 4

What must be defined in SAP Central Business Configuration prior to creating the organizational structure?
Note: There are 2 correct answers to this question.

  A. Fiscal Year Variant
  B. Group Currency
  C. Chart of Accounts
  D. Leading Ledger

Explanation:

Prior to creating the organizational structure in SAP Central Business Configuration, the following two items must be defined:

Fiscal Year Variant: The fiscal year variant is used to define the financial year of an organization. It specifies the number of posting periods in a financial year, the start and end dates of each posting period, and the closing periods. The fiscal year variant must be defined before creating the organizational structure because it determines the organization's financial reporting periods.
Group Currency: The group currency is the currency used for consolidating the financial statements of a group of companies. It is used to report the financial performance and position of the group to external stakeholders. The group currency must be defined before creating the organizational structure because it is an essential part of the organization's financial reporting.

Answer: A, B

Question: 5

Which business objects were initially released as part of the SAP One Domain Model?
Note: There are 2 correct answers to this question.

  A. Workforce Person
  B. Cost Centre
  C. Bank
  D. Material

Explanation:

Two business objects that were initially released as part of the SAP One Domain Model are:

Workforce Person: The Workforce Person business object is used to represent an employee in an organization. It contains information such as the employee's personal details, job position, and employment history. The Workforce Person object is used in various SAP solutions, including SAP Success Factors and SAP ERP HCM.

Cost Center: The Cost Center business object is used to represent a specific area of an organization that incurs costs. It is used to manage and monitor costs related to specific business activities or projects. The Cost Center object is used in various SAP solutions, including SAP ERP Financials and SAP S/4HANA.

Answer: A, B

Question: 6

Which of the following tools is used during the Fit to Standard Analysis process of SAP S/4HANA Cloud deployment?
Note: There are 2 correct answers to this question

A. SAP Best Practices Explorer
B. SAP Transformation Navigator
C. SAP Road Map Viewer
D. Product Availability Matrix
E. Code Inspector

Explanation:

During the Fit to Standard Analysis process of SAP S/4HANA Cloud deployment, two tools are commonly used:

SAP Best Practices Explorer: This tool provides preconfigured industry-specific and cross-industry business processes and solutions that can be used as a baseline for SAP S/4HANA Cloud deployment. The SAP Best Practices Explorer helps to identify the best practices that can be adopted and applied to the customer's business processes.

SAP Road Map Viewer: This tool provides a graphical representation of the recommended deployment process for SAP S/4HANA Cloud. It outlines the key milestones, tasks, and activities required for a successful deployment. The SAP Road Map Viewer helps to identify the areas where customization may be required to align the system with the customer's specific business requirements.

Answer: A, C

Question: 7

What is the service-level agreement (SLA) on corrective action for priority 1 incidents?

A. 6 hours, real time
B. 6 hours, office hours
C. 4 hours, office hours
D. 4 hours, real time

Explanation:

The service-level agreement (SLA) on corrective action for priority 1 incidents is 4 hours for real-time support. Priority 1 incidents are classified as critical issues that severely impact business operations, such as system outages or failures that affect multiple users. The SLA ensures that corrective action is taken as quickly as possible to minimize business disruption and restore normal system functionality.

In addition to the SLA on corrective action, there are also SLAs for response times and communication during the incident management process. For priority 1 incidents, the SLA for response time is also 4 hours for real-time support. The SLA for communication requires that regular updates are provided to the customer every 4 hours until the incident is resolved.

It's important to note that SLAs may vary depending on the specific terms and conditions of the customer's support contract with SAP.

Answer: D

Question: 8

What are the 4 pillars of SAP Preferred Care for SAP S/4HANA cloud?

 A. IT transformation road-map, On-Site support, project based offerings, and value assurance.
 B. Co-innovations, Business Operation Continuity, System Measurement and Expert chat
 C. Digital Transformation Support, Co-Development, Software Updates and Upgrades, and Knowledge Transfer
 D. Mission Critical Support, Collaboration Empowerment, and Innovation & Value Realization

Explanation:

The four pillars of SAP Preferred care for SAP S/4HANA Cloud are:

Mission Critical Support: This pillar focuses on ensuring that the customer's business-critical processes are operating as expected. It includes round-the-clock monitoring of the customer's systems, proactive identification of potential issues, and rapid resolution of critical incidents.
Collaboration Empowerment: This pillar aims to promote collaboration between the customer and SAP, to ensure that the customer is getting the most out of their SAP S/4HANA Cloud deployment. It includes regular meetings between the customer and SAP, access to SAP's best practices and expertise, and customized training to improve the customer's system usage.
Innovation & Value Realization: This pillar focuses on helping the customer continually innovate and drive value from their SAP S/4HANA Cloud investment. It includes access to SAP's innovation portfolio, assistance with implementing new features and functionality, and guidance on best practices for system optimization.

Trusted Advisor: This pillar provides the customer with a dedicated account manager who serves as a single point of contact for all SAP-related issues. The account manager works closely with the customer to understand their business needs, provide guidance on system usage, and ensure that the customer is getting the most out of their SAP S/4HANA Cloud investment.

Answer: D

Question: 9

What are the three value levers of the agility dimension?
Note: There are 3 correct answers to this question

A. Assimilate process innovation
B. Accelerate execution
C. Increase organizational agility
D. Increase process flexibility
E. Increase organizational speed

Explanation:

The three value levers of the agility dimension are:

Assimilate process innovation: This lever involves adopting new and innovative processes to improve agility. This could involve leveraging new technologies, streamlining existing processes, or adopting new business models.
Increase organizational agility: This lever focuses on increasing the ability of the organization to respond quickly to changing market conditions or customer needs. This could involve reorganizing teams, improving communication and collaboration, or implementing agile methodologies.
Increase process flexibility: This lever involves improving the flexibility of existing processes to accommodate changing business needs. This could involve simplifying processes, reducing dependencies, or improving automation.

Answer: A, C, D

Question: 10

Our machine learning use case is an example of which value lever dimension?

A. Increase agility
B. Assimilate process innovation
C. Increase efficiency
D. Increase effectiveness

Explanation:

The machine learning use case is an example of the "Increase Effectiveness" value lever dimension. This is because machine learning algorithms can be used to automate and optimize processes, leading to better decision-making and improved business outcomes. By leveraging machine learning, organizations can achieve better accuracy, higher throughput, and reduced costs, which ultimately leads to increased effectiveness in achieving business goals.

Answer: D

Question: 11

What are the main value drivers of SAP S/4HANA cloud?
Note: There are 3 correct answers to this question

A. High degree of customization
B. Rapid innovation cycles
C. Fast time to value
D. Open to any database
E. Simplification of consumption

Explanation:

The main value drivers of SAP S/4HANA cloud are:

Rapid innovation cycles: SAP S/4HANA cloud is designed to enable rapid innovation by providing regular updates and new features that can be easily adopted by customers.
Fast time to value: SAP S/4HANA cloud is designed to deliver fast time to value by providing preconfigured business processes, best practices, and simplified implementation tools.
Simplification of consumption: SAP S/4HANA cloud simplifies consumption by providing a cloud-based, subscription-based model that enables customers to pay for only what they use and easily scale up or down as needed.

By leveraging these value drivers, organizations can achieve benefits such as faster time-to-market, improved agility, and reduced IT complexity and costs. The high degree of customization and open to any database are not considered main value drivers of SAP S/4HANA Cloud, as the cloud offering is designed to provide standardization and reduce the need for customization, and it is optimized to run on the SAP HANA database.

Answer: B, C, E

Question: 12

What does public cloud stand for?
Note: There are 3 correct answers to this question

A. Scalability
B. Platform as a Service
C. Fully mobilized
D. Standardization
E. High degree of configuration

Explanation:

Public cloud refers to a cloud computing model where the cloud services are provided by a third-party provider and are made available to the general public over the internet.

Scalability: Public cloud services can easily scale up or down based on the user's demand, ensuring that the user only pays for the resources they consume.
Platform as a Service (PaaS): Public cloud providers offer PaaS, a cloud computing model where the provider offers a platform that enables users to develop, run, and manage their own applications without the need to manage the underlying infrastructure.
High degree of configuration: Public cloud providers offer a high degree of configuration, which allows users to customize their cloud environment to meet their specific needs.

Answer: A, B, E

Question: 13

Which of the following are possible steps towards making SAP S/4HANA cloud becomes a two-tier ERP deployment?
Note: There are 3 correct answers to this question

A. Ensure that reporting provides visibility in subsidiaries.
B. Implement all subsidiary-specific processes in your headquarter' ERP system.
C. Differentiate with integrated processes that you need to run between headquarters and subsidiaries
D. Integrate on the financial side by performing consolidation and corporate planning
E. Upgrade your headquarters' ERP system

Explanation:

A two-tier ERP deployment is a strategy where a company uses two ERP systems to manage their business operations. The headquarters typically has a larger, more complex ERP system, while smaller subsidiaries or business units use a simpler ERP system. SAP S/4HANA Cloud can be used as the subsidiary ERP system in a two-tier ERP deployment.

To make SAP S/4HANA Cloud a two-tier ERP deployment, there are several possible steps:

Ensure that reporting provides visibility in subsidiaries: This means that the headquarters' ERP system should be able to receive and consolidate data from the SAP S/4HANA Cloud systems used by subsidiaries. This will provide visibility into the operations of the subsidiaries, which is important for making strategic decisions.

Implement all subsidiary-specific processes in your headquarters' ERP system: To ensure consistency and reduce complexity, it is important to implement all subsidiary-specific processes in the headquarters' ERP system. This will also reduce the need for customization in the SAP S/4HANA Cloud systems used by subsidiaries.

Integrate on the financial side by performing consolidation and corporate planning: One of the key benefits of a two-tier ERP deployment is that it allows for better financial management and reporting. To take advantage of this, it is important to integrate financial data from subsidiaries into the headquarters' ERP system. This can be done through consolidation and corporate planning processes.

Answer: A, B, D

Question: 14

Which key elements does SAP Activate consist of?
Note: There are 3 correct answers to this question.

   A. Accelerated SAP (ASAP) B. Guided Configuration
   C. Simplification List
   D. Methodology
   E. SAP Best Practices

Explanation:

SAP Activate is a methodology used for the implementation of SAP S/4HANA and other SAP solutions. It consists of three key elements:

Guided Configuration: This is a step-by-step approach that guides users through the system configuration process. It allows users to tailor the system to their specific needs while still ensuring that best practices are followed.

Methodology: SAP Activate provides a framework for project management, including templates and tools for project planning, execution, and monitoring. It also includes guidance for change management, testing, and cutover activities.

SAP Best Practices: This is a preconfigured content library that includes business processes, configuration settings, and reports. It provides a baseline for system configuration and helps speed up the implementation process.

Answer: B, D, E

Question: 15

Which of the following tools are used during the Realize phase of an SAP S/4HANA Cloud deployment?
Note: There are 3 correct answers to this question

A. Test Tool
B. Implementation Guide (IMG) C. Product Availability Matrix
D. Migration Cockpit
E. Manage Your Solution Application

Explanation:

During the Realize phase of an SAP S/4HANA Cloud deployment, the following tools are commonly used:

Test Tool: The Test Tool allows users to plan, execute, and track testing during the realization phase. It enables users to define test scenarios, record test results, and track defects.
Implementation Guide (IMG): The Implementation Guide provides step-by-step instructions for setting up and configuring SAP S/4HANA Cloud. It includes a comprehensive list of configuration activities that must be performed to meet specific business requirements.
Product Availability Matrix (PAM): The Product Availability Matrix provides detailed information about which SAP products and versions are compatible with each other. It helps customers and partners to ensure that they have the correct product versions installed and configured to support their SAP S/4HANA Cloud deployment.
Migration Cockpit: The Migration Cockpit is a tool that is used to migrate data from legacy systems to SAP S/4HANA Cloud. It supports data migration for various functional areas, such as financials, logistics, and sales.
Manage Your Solution Application: The Manage Your Solution application is a cloud-based tool that allows users to manage their SAP S/4HANA Cloud solution. It provides a single entry point for managing incidents, changes, and service requests. Users can also access documentation and training materials through this application.

Answer: A, B, D

Question: 16

What is the right sequence for an SAP S/4HANA Cloud upgrade?

A. Q system upgrade → test phase → P system upgrade
B. P system upgrade → Q system upgrade → test phase
C. Test phase →Q system upgrade → P system upgrade
D. Q system upgrade → P system upgrade → test phase

Explanation:

The correct sequence for an SAP S/4HANA Cloud upgrade is Q system upgrade, test phase, and P system upgrade. This sequence ensures that any issues or errors discovered during the test phase can be addressed before the upgrade is performed on the production system (P system).

Option A is the correct sequence because the Q system, which is the quality assurance system, is upgraded first, followed by the test phase to ensure that the upgrade was successful and all the features are working as expected. Finally, the upgrade is performed on the production system (P system).

Answer: A

Question: 17

How many upgrades of your SAP S/4HANA Cloud system are you allowed to skip?

A. Two
B. Three
C. None
D. One

Explanation:

In SAP S/4HANA Cloud, you are not allowed to skip any upgrades. This means that once your system is upgraded to the latest version, you must keep it current by applying all future upgrades. Skipping upgrades can lead to compatibility issues, security vulnerabilities, and missing out on important new features and enhancements. It is recommended to plan ahead and allocate resources for each upgrade to ensure a smooth transition to the latest version.

Answer: C

Question: 18

What are the three value levers of the increased efficiency dimension?

A. Digital out-tasking
B. Up skill employees
C. Automate process steps
D. Accelerate execution
E. De-layer processes

Explanation:

The three value levers of the increased efficiency dimension are:

Digital out-tasking: This means outsourcing non-core processes and leveraging external expertise to improve the efficiency of the processes.

Automate process steps: This means using technologies such as robotic process automation (RPA) to automate repetitive tasks and improve the speed and accuracy of the processes.

Accelerate execution: This means optimizing end-to-end processes, reducing process handoffs, and improving the speed of execution.

While up skilling employees and de-layering processes may lead to increased efficiency, they are not specific value levers within the increased efficiency dimension.

Answer: A, C, D

Question: 19

Which of the following options helps to increase effectiveness in business practice?
Note: There are 3 correct answers to this question

A. Satisfy customers with new models
B. Lower maintenance costs
C. More value per employee
D. Fewer stock-outs
E. Operational excellence

Explanation:

Increasing effectiveness in business practice refers to achieving specific business outcomes, such as meeting customer demands, increasing productivity, reducing costs, and optimizing inventory levels. The following options can help to increase effectiveness in business practice:

- Satisfying customers with new models helps to increase the effectiveness of a business practice by increasing customer satisfaction and loyalty. This can lead to repeat business and positive word-of-mouth advertising, which ultimately drives growth and revenue.

- More value per employee means that employees are able to produce more output with the same amount of resources, resulting in increased efficiency and productivity. This leads to a higher return on investment for the company and ultimately increases its effectiveness.

- Fewer stock-outs mean that customers are able to get the products they need when they need them, which can increase customer satisfaction and ultimately drive revenue. This also helps to reduce the risk of lost sales and stock spoilage, which can impact the company's bottom line.

Answer: A, C, D

Question: 20

What are the main value drivers of SAP S/4HANA Cloud?
Note: There are 3 correct answers to this question.

A. High degree of customization
B. Rapid innovation cycles
C. Fast time to value
D. Open to any database
E. Simplification of consumption

Explanation:

The main value drivers of SAP S/4HANA cloud are as follows:

Rapid innovation cycles: SAP S/4HANA cloud is built on a modern in-memory platform that enables continuous innovation and provides the ability to quickly adapt to changing business needs. The platform also enables customers to take advantage of new technologies such as artificial intelligence (AI), machine learning (ML), and the Internet of Things (IoT).
Fast time to value: With preconfigured business processes and best practices, SAP S/4HANA cloud can be quickly deployed and configured to meet specific business needs, reducing the time and effort required to implement and operate the solution. This helps organizations achieve a faster return on investment (ROI) and realize the value of their investment sooner.
Simplification of consumption: SAP S/4HANA cloud provides a modern, user-friendly interface that is easy to use and requires minimal training. The solution also supports flexible deployment options; including public, private, and hybrid cloud deployments, as well as on-premise installations. This simplifies the consumption of the solution and enables customers to choose the deployment model that best suits their specific business needs.

Answer: B, C, E

Question: 21

What does "two-tier ERP system landscape of an SAP S/4HANA cloud deployment" mean?

A. Subsidiaries are managed by the headquarters' ERP system.
B. A backup ERP system is installed at the headquarters.
C. Subsidiaries run their own ERP system
D. Backup and archiving solutions are installed at each subsidiary.

Explanation:

The "two-tier ERP system landscape of an SAP S/4HANA Cloud deployment" means that a company uses two different ERP systems: the headquarters' ERP system and the subsidiary's own ERP system. In this scenario, the subsidiary runs its own ERP system, which is connected to the headquarters' ERP system. This approach is often used when the headquarters has complex, company-wide processes that need to be managed in a single ERP system, while subsidiaries have their own unique, local processes that are better managed in a separate ERP system. The two systems are integrated to allow for seamless communication and data exchange between headquarters and subsidiaries.

Answer: C

Question: 22

Why does SAP deliver country-specific versions of SAP S/4HANA Cloud?
Note: There are 3 correct answers to this question.

  A. To empower the business to run complaint locally and compete globally
  B. To facilitate deployment in local data centres
  C. To offer internationalization capabilities, such as Unicode compliance, currency support, time-zone adjustments, text processing using user locals, and more
  D. To offer the software in local languages
  E. To fulfil the export goals of the company

Explanation:

SAP delivers country-specific versions of SAP S/4HANA Cloud to empower businesses to run compliant locally and compete globally. This means that the system is localized to meet the specific legal and business requirements of each country or region where it is deployed.

Internationalization capabilities such as Unicode compliance, currency support, time-zone adjustments, text processing using user locals, and more are provided to make sure that the system works smoothly in various countries.

Furthermore, providing the software in local languages helps ensure that users can interact with the system in a way that is familiar and comfortable for them, thus increasing user adoption and productivity.

Answer: A, C, D

Question: 23

Which of the following finance capabilities are on the roadmap for the 1708 release of SAP S/4HANA Cloud?
Note: There are 2 correct answers to this question.

A. Bank Fee Analysis
B. Treasury and Risk Management
C. Cost Center Plan Allocation
D. Leveraging SAP Cloud Platform for finance
E. Financial Shared Services

Explanation:

In the 1708 release of SAP S/4HANA Cloud, two finance capabilities that were added to the system are Treasury and Risk Management and Financial Shared Services.

Treasury and Risk Management provide organizations with functionalities that enable them to manage various financial risks, such as market risks, credit risks, and liquidity risks. This capability helps organizations better predict future cash flows and make informed investment and financing decisions.

Financial Shared Services allow organizations to consolidate financial activities into one central location, streamlining financial processing and reducing the cost of the finance function. This capability can also enable better control and visibility over financial processes and provide more accurate and timely financial reporting.

Answer: B, E

Question: 24

Which of the following statements regarding the positioning of SAP S/4HANA Cloud and SAP Ariba are true?
Note: There are 3 correct answers to this question.

A. SAP S/4HANA Cloud covers operational procurement processes.
B. SAP Ariba provides operational procurement with tight integration to other business processes such as material requirements planning (MRP).
C. SAP Ariba provides network communication and strategic procurement.
D. SAP offers prebuilt integration for SAP Ariba and SAP S/4HANA Cloud.
E. SAP Ariba is required on top of SAP S/4HANA Cloud to do operational procurement.

Explanation:

SAP S/4HANA Cloud is positioned as a solution that covers operational procurement processes. This means that it is designed to handle the day-to-day purchasing activities such as creating purchase requisitions, purchase orders, and managing supplier invoices.

On the other hand, SAP Ariba is positioned as a solution that provides network communication and strategic procurement capabilities. This means that it is designed to enable businesses to connect with suppliers, manage supplier relationships, and conduct strategic sourcing activities like sourcing events and auctions.

SAP offers prebuilt integration for SAP Ariba and SAP S/4HANA Cloud, which means that businesses can easily connect the two solutions to achieve a unified procurement process. However, it's important to note that SAP Ariba is not required on top of SAP S/4HANA Cloud to do operational procurement. SAP S/4HANA Cloud can handle operational procurement processes on its own.

Answer: A, C, D

Question: 25

Which of the following processes uses predictive analytics in SAP S/4HANA cloud?

  A. Direct Materials Procurement
  B. Supplier Activities
  C. Invoice Matching
  D. Contract Consumption

Explanation:

The process that uses predictive analytics in SAP S/4HANA cloud is contract consumption. The contract consumption process uses predictive analytics to forecast future contract consumption and to identify potential deviations from the forecast. This helps companies optimize their contract utilization and reduce costs. By analyzing historical consumption data, the system can make predictions about future demand, taking into account seasonality, trends, and other factors. Based on these predictions, the system can recommend actions such as adjusting inventory levels, renegotiating contracts, or optimizing production planning. This allows companies to make more informed decisions and improve their bottom line.

Answer: D

Question: 26

In the unit on "Digital Order and Contract Management," what was one of the business priorities of SAP S/4HANA Cloud that was presented?

  A. Accelerated Plan to Product
  B. Core Finance
  C. Optimized Order to Cash
  D. Streamlined Procure to Pay

Explanation:

The business priority of SAP S/4HANA cloud presented in the unit was optimized order to cash. This refers to the process of managing sales orders, from creation to payment receipt, with the goal of improving efficiency, accuracy, and customer satisfaction. By streamlining this process, businesses can reduce errors, eliminate delays, and gain better visibility into customer behaviour and preferences. SAP S/4HANA Cloud provides a range of tools and capabilities to support optimized order to cash, including advanced analytics, real-time data processing, and mobile accessibility.

Answer: C

Question: 27

Which of the following best practices are included in the order and contract management end-to-end solution?
Note: There are 3 correct answers to this question.

A. Intercompany and Sales Order Processing (Domestic and International)
B. Accounts Receivable
C. Accelerated Customer Returns
D. Stock Handling
E. Advanced Available-to-Promise Processing (aATP)

Explanation:

The best practices included in the order and contract management end-to-end solution are Intercompany and sales order processing (Domestic and International), accelerated customer returns, and advanced available-to-promise processing (aATP).

- Intercompany and sales order processing cover the creation, management, and fulfilment of domestic and international sales orders, including intercompany transactions.
- Accelerated customer returns provide a streamlined and efficient process for managing customer returns.
- Advanced available-to-promise processing (aATP) provides real-time visibility into product availability and delivery dates, allowing for accurate order commitments and optimized fulfilment.

Answer: A, C, E

Question: 28

Which of the following are functions in the standard order to cash process?
Note: There are 3 correct answers to this question.

A. Subcontracting
B. Procurement of materials
C. Availability of the articles purchased
D. Calculation of pricing and taxes
E. Scheduling the delivery of goods

Explanation:

The order to cash process is a series of interconnected activities, starting with receiving a customer order and ending with receiving payment for the goods or services delivered. The standard functions of the order to cash process include:

Availability of the articles purchased: Before accepting the customer order, the system should check whether the requested articles are available in stock or whether they need to be produced or procured. This step ensures that the customer gets the desired goods or services on time.

Calculation of pricing and taxes: Once the requested articles are confirmed as available, the system should calculate the pricing based on the customer-specific pricing agreements, discounts, and surcharges. Also, the system should calculate the taxes based on country-specific tax laws and regulations.

Scheduling the delivery of goods: After the pricing and taxes are calculated, the system should schedule the delivery of goods to the customer based on the requested delivery date, the transport mode, and the availability of the delivery resources.

Answer: C, D, E

Question: 29

Which of the following business priorities is covered by the end-to-end process for professional services?
Note: There are 3 correct answers to this question.

  A. Accelerated Plan to Product
  B. Core Finance
  C. Project Services
  D. Optimized Order to Cash
  E. Inventory Management

Explanation:

The end-to-end process for professional services covers the business priorities of core finance; project services, and optimized order to cash. Core finance is important for accounting and financial reporting, while project services include the management of resources, billing, and profitability analysis.

Optimized order to cash focuses on efficient and accurate order processing, delivery, and payment collection. The other options, accelerated plan to product and inventory management, are not directly related to the end-to-end process for professional services.

Answer: B, C, D

Question: 30

Which end-to-end solutions are mapped to the project services business priority?
Note: There are 3 correct answers to this question.

  A. Project management
  B. Time and expense management
  C. Maintenance management
  D. Contract to cash
  E. HR connectivity

Explanation:

The project services business priority focuses on the management of projects and related activities. The end-to-end solutions that are mapped to this priority are project management, time and expense management, and contract to cash.

Project management involves planning, executing, and monitoring projects to ensure they are completed within the defined scope, budget, and timeline. Time and expense management helps track the time and expenses incurred by resources working on a project. This allows for accurate billing of clients and effective cost management.

Contract to Cash covers the entire process from contract creation to payment collection for services rendered. It includes elements such as project billing, revenue recognition, and customer billing.

Answer: A, B, D

Question: 31

Which of the following business priorities in SAP S/4HANA cloud focuses on production capabilities?

  A. Optimized order to cash
  B. project service
  C. HR connectivity
  D. Accelerated plan to product

Explanation:

The business priority of SAP S/4HANA Cloud that focuses on production capabilities is "Accelerated Plan to Product." This priority is concerned with improving the planning, manufacturing, and delivery of products by optimizing supply chain processes, reducing production cycle times, and enhancing collaboration across departments. It includes end-to-end solutions for managing procurement, manufacturing, inventory, and logistics operations. By streamlining production processes, organizations can improve their ability to respond to customer demand, increase operational efficiency, and reduce costs.

Answer: D

Question: 32

Which of the following process steps is included in the make to stock process?

  A. Create sales order
  B. Check or preview purchase order
  C. Create return delivery
  D. Create production order

Explanation:

The make to stock process involves producing goods based on demand forecasts, with the aim of keeping a certain amount of stock on hand to fulfil customer orders. In this process, the creation of a production order is a crucial step that initiates the manufacturing process of the finished product. This production order specifies the quantity of the product to be produced, the location of the production, the resources required, and the time frame for production.

Answer: D

Question: 33

How can you model company-specific data access on top of public CDS views in SAP S/4HANA Cloud?

  A. By using the Query browser app
  B. By modelling inside the ABAP for Eclipse environment
  C. By using the Custom CDS View app (view modeller)
  D. By using the CDS View Browser app

Explanation:

In SAP S/4HANA cloud, you can model company-specific data access on top of public core data services (CDS) views using the Custom CDS View app, also known as the view modeller. This app allows you to create custom CDS views that are based on existing public CDS views and tailored to your company's specific needs.

You can add additional fields, filters, and calculations to the view and define data access restrictions based on organizational units, roles, or other criteria. By using the custom CDS view app, you can extend the standard data models provided by SAP and create a more flexible and tailored data access layer for your organization.

Answer: C

Question: 34

What do business users request today?
Note: There are 3 correct answers to this question.

  A. Advanced analytical capabilities
  B. Separate front ends for analytics and transactions
  C. Real-time insight in their SAP S/4HANA system
  D. One report for all business requests
  E. Contextual information along their transactions

Explanation:

Business user's today request advanced analytical capabilities, real-time insight into their SAP S/4HANA system, and contextual information along with their transactions. This means that they need more than just simple reports, but rather sophisticated analysis tools that allow them to analyze data and gain insights quickly and easily. They also need to be able to access this information in real-time, so they can make informed decisions on the spot. Additionally, users need to have relevant information available to them within the context of their transactions, to make more informed decisions.

Answer: A, C, E

Question: 35

How can you get an overview of the entire Core data services (CDS) views in SAP S/4HANA embedded analytics?

  A. Use the View Browser app.
  B. Use the Query Browser app.
  C. Use the ABAP Dictionary and search for the term "query".
  D. Use the Multi dimensional reporting client.

Explanation:

The View Browser app provides an overview of all the available Core Data Services (CDS) views in SAP S/4HANA embedded analytics. It allows users to search for CDS views by name or description and also filter them by different criteria, such as business area, author, or creation date. Additionally, the View Browser app displays relevant metadata for each CDS view, such as the name of the underlying database table, the list of fields and their data types, and the annotations used for semantic and UI modelling.

Answer: A

Question: 36

What is the easiest way to familiarize you with SAP S/4HANA embedded analytics?

A. Install an on-premise SAP S/4HANA system.
B. Use the SAP S/4HANA Cloud trial online.
C. Use an existing SAP BW/4HANA system.
D. Download all analytics solutions delivered by SAP.

Explanation:

The easiest way to familiarize you with SAP S/4HANA embedded analytics is to use the SAP S/4HANA cloud trial online. This option provides access to a fully functional SAP S/4HANA system without the need for installation or additional hardware.

The trial environment is preconfigured with sample data and provides access to various apps and tools, including embedded analytics, to explore the functionality and features of the system. This allows users to gain practical experience with SAP S/4HANA embedded analytics before deciding to implement it in their organization.

Answer: B

Question: 37

Where can you create custom-specific apps for your SAP S/4HANA Cloud?

A. Only in SAP S/4HANA Cloud as in-app extensions
B. In SAP S/4HANA Cloud or on SAP Cloud Platform
C. Only on SAP Cloud Platform as side-by-side extensions
D. Custom-specific apps are not allowed in SAP S/4HANA Cloud

Explanation:

Custom-specific apps for SAP S/4HANA cloud can be created both in SAP S/4HANA cloud as in-app extensions and on the SAP cloud platform. In-app extensions are created and managed within SAP S/4HANA cloud, while side-by-side extensions are created and managed on the SAP cloud platform and can be integrated with SAP S/4HANA cloud. This provides flexibility for customers to extend the standard SAP S/4HANA cloud functionality according to their business requirements.

Answer: B

Question: 38

How can you make your custom field searchable in free-text search?

A. Use the search setting in SAP Fiori launch pad
B. Check the Search Relevance checkbox in the UIs and Reports section of the Custom Fields and Logic app
C. Use the search setting in the Custom CDS Views app
D. Use the UI Adaptation Mode app

Explanation:

To make a custom field searchable in free-text search, you need to check the "Search Relevance" checkbox in the UIs and reports section of the custom fields and Logic app. This will allow the custom field to be included in the free-text search index, which enables users to search for data using keywords or phrases. By default, custom fields are not included in the free-text search index, so it is important to enable this setting if you want to make your custom field searchable.

Answer: B

Question: 39

Why do SAP-delivered integrations enable customers to achieve maximum speed to value?
Note: There are 3 correct answers to this question.

A. Because SAP Cloud to SAP Cloud integrations are pre-delivered with best practices content delivered by SAP
B. Because they are operated by customers
C. Because they are predefined and developed by SAP
D. Because new developments and upgrades are performed by the customers
E. Because they are operated by SAP

Explanation:

SAP-delivered integrations enable customers to achieve maximum speed to value for several reasons. First, SAP cloud to SAP cloud integrations are pre-delivered with best practices content delivered by SAP, which means that customers can quickly and easily connect their SAP systems without having to develop custom integrations.
Second, these integrations are predefined and developed by SAP, which means that they are built using the latest technologies and best practices.
Finally, SAP-operated integrations are managed and operated by SAP, which ensures that they are always up-to-date and fully supported, freeing customers from the burden of managing and maintaining their integrations.

Answer: A, C, E

Question: 40

To which of the following systems does SAP provide pre-delivered integration with SAP S/4HANA?
Note: There are 3 correct answers to this question.

A. SAP Concur
B. SAP Success Factors
C. SAP Ariba
D. SAP Human Capital Management
E. Third-party systems for managing travel and expenses

Explanation:

SAP provides pre-delivered integration with three systems, namely SAP Concur, SAP Success Factors, and SAP Ariba. These integrations are designed to simplify the integration process for customers and ensure a faster time-to-value.
SAP Concur is a travel and expense management system, SAP Success Factors is an HR management system, and SAP Ariba is a procurement and supply chain management system.

Answer: A, B, C

Question: 41

Why is it easy to create new workflows in SAP S/4HANA Cloud?
Note: There are 3 correct answers to this question.

A. Because you can use the intuitive SAP Fiori 2.0 design
B. Because there is no technical know-how needed to set up a new workflow
C. Because you can create alternative, simple workflows instead of large, error-prone workflows
D. Because you can use the intuitive ARIS Toolset
E. Because loops, branches, and thresholds for workflow steps are determined automatically without user interaction

Explanation:

One reason it is easy to create new workflows in SAP S/4HANA Cloud is that you can use the intuitive SAP Fiori 2.0 design, which provides a user-friendly interface for designing workflows. Additionally, there is no technical know-how needed to set up a new workflow, as the system provides templates and pre-built workflows that can be easily customized to fit your needs.
Another advantage is that you can create alternative, simple workflows instead of large, error-prone workflows, allowing you to better control and manage the process. This helps to ensure that workflows are efficient and effective while minimizing the risk of errors or delays.

Answer: A, B, C

Question: 42

Which of the following are functions of output management in SAP S/4HANA cloud?
Note: There are 3 correct answers to this question.

  A. Updating multiple master data records at a time
  B. Entering a recipient
  C. Choosing the output method such as print, fax, or e-mail
  D. Assigning workflows
  E. Previewing a document

Explanation:

Output management in SAP S/4 HANA cloud is responsible for generating and distributing business documents to recipients in different formats, such as print, fax, or email. It enables users to control the way business documents are created, formatted, and distributed to different recipients. Some of the functions of output management in SAP S/4HANA cloud include:

- Entering a recipient: Users can select the recipient(s) for the output document, such as a customer, vendor, or employee.
- Choosing the output method: Users can choose the output method for the document, such as print, fax, or email. This helps to ensure that the document is sent to the correct recipient in the format they require.
- Previewing a document: Users can preview the output document before sending it to the recipient. This helps to ensure that the document looks correct and contains the required information.

Other functions of output management may include assigning workflows, updating multiple master data records at a time, and creating variants for different document types. By providing these functions, output management in SAP S/4 HANA cloud helps organizations streamline their business processes, improve efficiency, and reduce errors.

Answer: B, C, E

Question: 43

Which of the following are characteristics of the analytics solutions for SAP S/4HANA cloud?
Note: There are 3 correct answers to this question.

  A. They require an additional deployment of business intelligence front ends
  B. They provide instant insight to action
  C. They provide data warehouse functionality
  D. They provide KPI visualization and modelling apps

E. They support process execution through contextualized information

Explanation:

The analytics solutions for SAP S/4HANA cloud provide three main characteristics:

- Instant insight to action: Analytics solutions provide real-time data analysis that enables users to make informed decisions quickly. With the help of analytics solutions, users can create meaningful insights from their data to drive their business forward.
- KPI visualization and modeling apps: Analytics solutions come with pre-built KPI models that allow users to monitor and track business performance against their goals. These models can be customized to meet specific business requirements.
- Support process execution through contextualized information: Analytics solutions provide users with relevant and contextualized information that supports their business processes. For example, they can provide users with insights into supplier performance, which can help them, make better purchasing decisions.

In contrast to the above, analytics solutions do not require an additional deployment of business intelligence front ends and do not provide data warehouse functionality.

Answer: B, D, E

Question: 44

Which of the following tasks can you perform on an Analytical List page?

- A. Dig into KPIs, Overview pages, and transactions
- B. Modify the data models
- C. Define KPIs
- D. Create and manage analytical queries

Explanation:

An Analytical list page in SAP S/4HANA Cloud provides a real-time overview of key performance indicators (KPIs) and transactional data in a list format. On the Analytical List Page, users can dig into the KPIs, Overview pages, and transactions to get insights and make informed decisions.

However, modifying the data models or defining KPIs are not tasks that can be performed directly on the Analytical List Page. These tasks require more advanced configuration and customization in other applications, such as the Custom CDS Views app or the KPI Modeling app.

Creating and managing analytical queries is also not a task that can be performed directly on the

Analytical List Page. However, the Analytical List Page provides a way to display the results of predefined analytical queries created in other applications, such as the Query Designer app or the Custom CDS Views app.

Answer: A

Question: 45

Which of the following tasks can you perform using the event based revenue recognition app?
Note: There are 3 correct answers to this question.

A. Launch a separate SAP Analytics Cloud report
B. Analyze individual recognition postings
C. Adjust the recognized revenue and cost of sales
D. Enter accruals
E. Pick values from a list of predicted and weighted results

Explanation:

The Event-Based Revenue Recognition app is designed to perform revenue recognition tasks based on the occurrence of certain events, such as the delivery of goods or completion of services. With this app, you can analyze individual recognition postings, which is one of the tasks that can be performed using the app. This allows you to review the recognition postings and ensure that they are accurate and in compliance with accounting standards.

You can also enter accruals using the Event-Based Revenue Recognition app. Accruals are adjustments made to the financial statements to reflect expenses or revenue that have been incurred or earned but not yet recorded. This feature allows you to make adjustments to the revenue recognition process, which can help ensure that your financial statements are accurate.

Answer: B, D

Question: 46

Which of the following tasks can you perform using in-app extensibility applications in SAP S/4HANA cloud?
Note: There are 3 correct answers to this question.

A. Define custom CDS views for your analytical requirements
B. Add custom fields to screens, forms, or APIs
C. Develop add-ons
D. Add business logic, for example in a BAdI
E. Change the format of dates and numbers

Explanation:

In-app extensibility applications in SAP S/4HANA cloud allow users to extend the system's functionality in a non-disruptive manner. These applications provide the ability to perform various tasks, such as adding custom fields to screens, forms, or APIs to capture additional data, defining custom CDS views for analytical requirements, and adding business logic to modify or enhance the standard behaviour of the system.

Changing the format of dates and numbers is not a task that can be performed using in-app extensibility, but can be achieved using other tools such as Custom Fields and Logic app. Developing add-ons typically requires more extensive customization and is not considered an in-app extensibility task.

Answer: A, B, D

Question: 47

Which of the following apps do you use to define a new field (in-app extensibility) for screens, forms, or APIs?

A. Custom CDS Views
B. Custom Fields and Logic
C. UI Adaptation Mode
D. Custom Business Objects

Explanation:

To define a new field in SAP S/4HANA cloud for screens, forms, or APIs, you would use the Custom Fields and Logic app, which is part of the in-app extensibility framework. This app allows you to add custom fields to standard screens and forms, as well as to APIs, in a non-disruptive way.

The Custom Fields and Logic app provides a user-friendly interface to create custom fields and define the data types, values, and business rules for these fields. You can also set up dependencies between fields, perform validations, and customize the UI presentation for the fields.

Once the custom field is created, it can be used in standard reports and forms, and can be accessed via the APIs. This allows you to capture additional data that is specific to your business needs without having to make extensive customizations to the system.

Answer: B

Question: 48

Which types of integration are provided with SAP S/4HANA cloud?
Note: There are 3 correct answers to this question.

A. Template-based integrations
B. Integration of lines of business and IT teams
C. SAP solutions with SAP-delivered productized integrations
D. Customer-driven integrations with APIs provided by SAP
E. Mergers and acquisitions integration

Explanation:

SAP S/4HANA Cloud provides various integration options to connect with other systems and solutions. Template-based integrations enable quick integration with other SAP solutions, while SAP offers productized integrations with its own solutions to ensure reliable and optimized integrations.

Customers can also use the APIs provided by SAP to build their own integrations to meet their specific business needs. Mergers and acquisitions integration may require integration between SAP S/4HANA cloud and other systems, but it is not a type of integration provided by SAP S/4HANA cloud itself.

Answer: A, C, D

Question: 49

Which of the following statements regarding customer-driven integration is true?

A. SAP Cloud Platform Integration cannot be used for customer-driven integration
B. Customer-driven integration is operated by SAP
C. Customer-driven integration requires that the integration is scoped and built based on APIs provided by SAP
D. Customer-driven integration enables you to achieve maximum speed to value

Explanation:

Customer-driven integration is a type of integration that enables customers to build their own integrations to connect SAP S/4HANA Cloud with other systems, such as non-SAP applications. This type of integration is designed to give customers flexibility and control over how their systems are integrated with SAP S/4HANA Cloud, allowing them to meet their specific business requirements.
To build a customer-driven integration, customers must first scope and plan the integration according to their specific needs. This involves identifying the data and functionality that needs to be integrated, as well as any business rules or requirements that must be met. Once the integration is scoped, customers can then develop the integration using APIs provided by SAP.

APIs, or application programming interfaces, are a set of protocols and tools used to build software applications. SAP provides a range of APIs that customers can use to access data and functionality within SAP S/4HANA Cloud. These APIs allow customers to integrate SAP S/4HANA Cloud with other systems, such as non-SAP applications, in a way that is tailored to their specific business requirements.

While customer-driven integration provides customers with a high level of flexibility and customization, building a custom integration can require time and resources. As such, it may not always be the fastest way to achieve value. However, customer-driven integration allows customers to build integrations that are tailored to their specific business requirements, which can provide significant benefits in terms of efficiency, accuracy, and productivity.

Answer: C

Question: 50

What is the role of the workflow engine in SAP S/4HANA Cloud?

A. To import workflows generated with third-party workflow toolsets
B. To generate alternative, simple workflows from complex, error-prone workflows
C. To run, control, and monitor all workflow-related activities in the system
D. To transform flow charts and graphics into executable workflows

Explanation:

The workflow engine in SAP S/4HANA Cloud plays a critical role in managing all workflow-related activities in the system. This includes running, controlling, and monitoring workflows to ensure that tasks are completed efficiently and accurately.

The workflow engine is responsible for executing predefined business processes, known as workflows, which are designed to automate and streamline tasks across the organization. These workflows can include everything from simple approval processes to complex, multi-step processes involving multiple departments or systems.

The workflow engine provides a central location for managing workflows and associated tasks, allowing users to easily monitor the status of tasks and workflows, view pending tasks, and take action as needed. This helps to ensure that tasks are completed on time and according to the established business rules and requirements.
Overall, the workflow engine is a critical component of SAP S/4HANA Cloud, enabling organizations to automate and streamline their business processes, improve efficiency and productivity, and ensure compliance with established policies and procedures.

Answer: C

Question: 51

Which technology is used for output management in SAP S/4HANA Cloud?

A. Adobe Document Server and Adobe Forms
B. SAP Document Center

C. HP Document Server
D. SAP Cloud Platform Portal

Explanation:

Adobe Document Server and Adobe Forms are the technologies used for output management in SAP S/4HANA Cloud. These technologies enable organizations to generate and manage a wide range of business documents, including invoices, purchase orders, and shipping documents, among others. The

Adobe Forms are used to create templates for these documents, while the Adobe Document Server is used to generate and distribute them to the relevant stakeholders. This approach allows organizations to create and manage complex business documents more efficiently, while also ensuring that they are consistent in terms of format and content.

Answer: A

Question: 52

Which of the following are some of the key capabilities of SAP S/4HANA Cloud?
Note: There are 3 correct answers to this question.

   A. Distributed storage management
   B. Workflow
   C. Master data management
   D. Output management
   E. Web server management

Explanation:

SAP S/4HANA Cloud has several key capabilities that enable organizations to run their business operations efficiently. These include:

Workflow: The workflow engine in SAP S/4HANA Cloud allows organizations to create and manage workflows for various business processes. This helps to automate tasks, reduce manual effort, and improve process efficiency.

Master Data Management: SAP S/4HANA Cloud provides a centralized platform for managing master data across the organization. This includes data related to customers, vendors, products, and more. By maintaining accurate and consistent master data, organizations can improve decision-making, reduce errors, and improve overall business performance.

Output Management: With SAP S/4HANA Cloud, organizations can manage their business documents and correspondence efficiently. The solution provides capabilities for document creation, processing, and distribution, enabling organizations to streamline their document-related processes and reduce manual effort.

Overall, these capabilities help organizations to operate more efficiently and effectively, enabling them to focus on strategic activities and drive business growth.

Answer: B, C, D

Question: 53

What kind of enterprise is the company described in the case study presented in this unit?

A. A bicycle producer located in the United States
B. A global manufacturing enterprise
C. A distribution company located in Germany
D. A consulting company in the manufacturing industry

Explanation:

A bicycle producer located in the United States is described in the case study.

Answer: A

Question: 54

What are some of the challenges that Velotics is facing?
Note: There are 3 correct answers to this question.

A. Each of their lines of business is either working off spreadsheets or has its own insular, small-scale LoB application
B. They must convert from an existing SAP ERP system to SAP S/4HANA Cloud
C. They must add an accessories product line with products produced in-house as well as procured products to complement their cycle's line of business
D. Their current system does not support e-bikes master data
E. They do not have an IT department

Explanation:

Velotics is facing several challenges that are hindering its growth and operational efficiency. These challenges include:

Data management: Each of their lines of business is either working off spreadsheets or has its own insular, small-scale LoB application. This makes it difficult for the company to have a unified view of its operations and leads to inefficiencies in managing data. Velotics needs a centralized system that can provide real-time visibility into its operations, enabling better decision-making.
New product line: Velotics must add an accessories product line with products produced in-house as well as procured products to complement their line of business. This requires significant planning, investment, and effort to ensure that the new product line integrates well with existing processes and

systems. Velotics needs to identify and address any potential gaps or conflicts that may arise with the addition of the new product line.

IT expertise: Velotics does not have an IT department, which means they lack in-house expertise and resources to manage their systems and address any IT-related issues that arise. This puts the company at a disadvantage in terms of technology innovation and operational efficiency. Velotics needs to invest in IT expertise to manage and optimize their systems and stay competitive in the market.

System upgrade: Velotics needs to convert from an existing SAP ERP system to SAP S/4HANA Cloud. This is a complex and time-consuming process that requires careful planning and execution. Velotics needs to ensure that the migration is seamless and does not disrupt its operations.

E-bikes master data: Velotics' current system does not support e-bikes master data. With the growing demand for e-bikes, Velotics needs to ensure that its system can support this product line and capture the necessary data to make informed business decisions.

Addressing these challenges will require a significant investment of time, resources, and expertise, but it is essential for Velotics to overcome them to remain competitive in the market and achieve its business objectives.

Answer: A, C, E

Question: 55

Which of the following sources provides customers with useful information for the prepare and Discover phases of an SAP S/4HANA Cloud implementation project?
Note: There are 3 correct answers to this question.

A. SAP S/4HANA Cloud Simplification List
B. SAP S/4HANA Feature Scope Description
C. SAP S/4HANA Cloud Release Information
D. SAP S/4HANA Cloud Use Case Series
E. SAP S/4HANA Cloud Installation Guide

Explanation:

The sources that provide customers with useful information for the Prepare and Discover phases of an SAP S/4HANA Cloud implementation project are

SAP S/4HANA Feature Scope Description: This document provides customers with an overview of the features and functionalities of SAP S/4HANA Cloud. It outlines the business processes that are supported by the solution and the scope of the implementation project. This information is useful during the Prepare phase to help customers understand the capabilities of the solution and determine which features are relevant to their business needs.

SAP S/4HANA Cloud Release Information: This source provides customers with detailed information about the latest release of SAP S/4HANA Cloud. It includes information about new features and enhancements, as well as any changes to existing functionality. This information is useful during the Discover phase to help customers understand how the latest release can benefit their business and plan for any necessary system changes or updates.

SAP S/4HANA Cloud Use Case Series: This series of documents provides customers with real-world use cases and scenarios that demonstrate how SAP S/4HANA Cloud can be used to solve common business challenges. This information is useful during the Prepare and Discover phases to help customers understand how the solution can be applied to their specific business needs and processes.

SAP S/4HANA Cloud Simplification List: This document provides customers with information about the simplifications and changes that have been made to the solution in the latest release. It helps customers understand how these changes may impact their existing systems and processes. While it is useful during the Discover phase, it may not be as relevant during the Prepare phase.

SAP S/4HANA Cloud Installation Guide: This source provides technical information about the installation and configuration of SAP S/4HANA Cloud. While it is useful during the Implement phase of the project, it may not be as relevant during the Prepare and Discover phases.

Answer: B, C, D

Question: 56

What are the main tools that you are recommended to use during the explore phase of an SAP S/4HANA Cloud implementation project?
Note: There are 2 correct answers to this question.

  A. SAP Solution Builder
  B. ABAP Workbench
  C. SAP S/4HANA Cloud starter system
  D. SAP Best Practices Explorer

Explanation:

During the Explore phase of an SAP S/4HANA Cloud implementation project, the main tools recommended to use are the SAP S/4HANA Cloud starter system and SAP Best Practices Explorer.

The SAP S/4HANA Cloud starter system is a preconfigured system that allows teams to explore the functionality and capabilities of SAP S/4HANA Cloud in a sandbox environment. This system allows teams to test various scenarios and processes, and gain a better understanding of how the system works.

The SAP Best Practices Explorer is an online tool that provides access to a library of preconfigured business processes, which can be used as a reference during the Explore phase. This tool provides best practices and guidance for various business scenarios and can help teams identify the best way to configure the system for their specific needs.

Answer: C, D

Question: 57

Which of the following are accelerators at the scope item level that SAP provides with SAP Best Practices explorer for your SAP S/4HANA Cloud solution?
Note: There are 3 correct answers to this question.

A. Process diagrams
B. Prerequisites matrix
C. Scope-item fact sheets
D. Roadmap presentation
E. Test scripts

Explanation:

The accelerators at the scope item level that SAP provides with SAP Best Practices Explorer for the SAP S/4HANA Cloud solution are:

Process diagrams: These are visual representations of business processes that help users understand the flow of activities involved in a particular process.
Prerequisites matrix: This is a matrix that lists the prerequisites for a particular scope item, such as required settings or configurations.
Scope-item fact sheets: These provide detailed information about each scope item, including its purpose, key features, and configuration details.
Roadmap presentation: This is a presentation that outlines the recommended approach for implementing the SAP S/4HANA Cloud solution, including key milestones and activities.
Test scripts: These are preconfigured test scripts that can be used to test the functionality of a particular scope item, ensuring that it is working as expected.

Answer: A, C, E

Question: 58

What is the leading principle of guided configuration?

A. It is done by one line of business on behalf of another line of business
B. It can be done by key users in the lines of business without the support of a central IT department
C. It is done by line-of-business executives
D. It is done by IT consultants from the IT department

Explanation:

The leading principle of guided configuration is that it can be done by key users in the line of business without the support of a central IT department. Guided configuration is designed to be user-friendly and intuitive, allowing non-technical users to configure the SAP S/4HANA Cloud system to meet their specific business needs.

With guided configuration, key users can take ownership of the configuration process and make changes quickly and easily without having to rely on IT consultants or a central IT department. This helps to streamline the configuration process and ensure that the system is configured to meet the unique needs of each line of business.

Answer: B

Question: 59

Which of the following system configurations is protected by content lifecycle management against unwanted changes?
Note: There are 3 correct answers to this question.

  A. Personalization done by the customer
  B. New process steps and processes added by customers or partners
  C. System languages
  D. Currencies
  E. Pre-configuration delivered by SAP

Explanation:

Content Lifecycle Management (CLM) is a feature in SAP S/4HANA Cloud that protects system configurations against unwanted changes. The following system configurations are protected by CLM:

Personalization done by the customer: Personalization refers to changes made to the user interface or other aspects of the system that are specific to a particular user or group of users. These changes are protected by CLM to ensure that they are not overwritten by subsequent updates or changes to the system.

New process steps and processes added by customers or partners: Customers or partners may add new process steps or processes to the system to meet their specific business needs. These additions are protected by CLM to ensure that they are not inadvertently removed or modified by subsequent updates.

Pre-configuration delivered by SAP: SAP delivers pre-configured content to the system to help customers get started quickly. This pre-configuration is protected by CLM to ensure that it is not modified or overwritten by subsequent updates or changes to the system.

Answer: A, B, E

Question: 60

Which of the following are phases in both system lifecycle and SAP activate?
Note: There are 3 correct answers to this question.

A. Realize
B. Explore
C. Preset
D. Deploy
E. Change

Explanation:

System lifecycle and SAP Activate are two methodologies used in SAP projects. Both methodologies share some common phases, including:

Realize: This phase involves configuring and testing the system to ensure that it meets the requirements and specifications gathered during the previous phases.
Explore: This phase involves defining the scope of the project, gathering requirements, and identifying the best approach for implementing the SAP solution.
Deploy: This phase involves moving the system from the development environment to the production environment, testing it again, and performing user training.

Answer: A, B, D

Question: 61

From where can you download the SAP S/4HANA Cloud migration templates?

A. From the SAP S/4HANA migration cockpit
B. From SAP Help Portal
C. From SAP Cloud Platform
D. From SAP Service Marketplace

Explanation:

The SAP S/4HANA Cloud migration templates can be downloaded from the SAP S/4HANA migration cockpit. The migration cockpit is a tool provided by SAP that simplifies and automates the process of migrating data from a legacy system to SAP S/4HANA Cloud.

The migration templates provide predefined templates for migrating data from various source systems, such as SAP ERP, SAP CRM, and third-party systems. These templates are available in the migration cockpit and can be downloaded and customized as needed for specific migration projects.

Answer: A

Question: 62

When using the SAP S/4HANA migration cockpit, where can you find details regarding the structure of the fields in your migration objects, such as type and length?

A. In the downloaded migration template
B. In the system help of the cloud system
C. In the online help for the migration tool
D. In the individual object documentation

Explanation:

When using the SAP S/4HANA migration cockpit, details regarding the structure of the fields in your migration objects, such as type and length, can be found in the downloaded migration template. The migration template provides a structure for the data to be migrated, including field names, data types, and lengths. These details are defined in the template and can be customized as needed for specific migration projects.

It is important to review and understand the structure of the fields in the migration objects before beginning the data migration process, as this can help ensure the accuracy and completeness of the migrated data.

Answer: A

Question: 63

Which of the following are activities in an SAP S/4HANA cloud implementation that require key users' involvement?
Note: There are 3 correct answers to this question.

A. End-user training and on boarding
B. Cloud subscription fees monitoring
C. Accounts payable clearing
D. System personalization and configuration
E. Solution discovery

Explanation:

In an SAP S/4HANA cloud implementation, the following activities require key users' involvement:

End-user training and on boarding: Key users are responsible for ensuring that end-users are trained on how to use the new system and on boarded properly. They can create training materials, conduct training sessions, and provide ongoing support to end-users.

System personalization and configuration: Key users play a crucial role in configuring the system to meet their specific business requirements. They can use guided configuration to make changes to the system without the need for technical expertise, such as defining organizational structures, creating new fields, and customizing reports.

Solution discovery: Key users are often involved in the initial phase of the project, where they help identify the business requirements and recommend the best approach for implementing the SAP solution. They can work with business stakeholders to gather requirements and document the processes that need to be supported by the new system.

Answer: A, D, E

Question: 64

Which of the following applications is embedded in SAP S/4HANA cloud?
Note: There are 3 correct answers to this question.

A. SAP Learning Hub
B. Migration app
C. Configuration apps
D. Test app
E. SAP Best Practices Explorer

Explanation:

The following applications are embedded in SAP S/4HANA Cloud:

Migration app: The migration app is a tool that simplifies and automates the process of migrating data from a legacy system to SAP S/4HANA Cloud. It provides predefined templates for migrating data from various source systems and guides users through the migration process.

Configuration apps: These apps are used to configure the system to meet specific business requirements. They provide guided configuration options that allow users to make changes to the system without the need for technical expertise.

Test app: The test app is used to test the system after it has been configured and customized. It provides predefined test scenarios and test scripts to help ensure that the system is functioning as expected.

Answer: B, C, D

Question: 65

After you have reviewed the best practice process flow and demonstrated the business scenarios and concepts, what should you do next in a Fit to Standard workshop?

A. Provide process flows, test scripts, and users.

B. Enable the customer to execute the scenarios on their own.
C. Discuss how the processes fit with customer requirements.
D. Identify the required configuration.

Explanation:

After reviewing the best practice process flow and demonstrating business scenarios and concepts in a Fit to Standard workshop, the next step is to discuss how the processes fit with customer requirements.
This involves reviewing the gaps between the standard processes and the customer's specific requirements and identifying any customization or configuration that may be needed to meet those requirements. The goal is to find a balance between adopting the standard processes to the greatest extent possible and meeting the customer's specific needs.

Answer: C

Question: 66

Which of the following statements regarding the starter system for SAP S/4HANA Cloud is true?
Note: There are 3 correct answers to this question.

A. It is provided by the SAP service center.
B. You can transport your configuration in the starter system to your Q and P systems.
C. It contains master data.
D. It contains your required configuration.
E. It contains model company configuration.

Explanation:

The following statements regarding the starter system for SAP S/4HANA Cloud are true:

- It is provided by the SAP service center.
- It contains master data, which is preconfigured data that is needed for business transactions.
- It contains model company configuration, which provides an example of best practices and can be used as a basis for configuring the system to meet the needs of a specific customer.

It is important to note that the starter system is not intended for use in a production environment, but rather as a testing and development environment. You can transport your configuration from the starter system to your Q and P systems, which are the quality assurance and production environments, respectively.

Answer: A, C, E

Question: 67

In which of the following system lifecycle phases is the Q-system used?
Note: There are 3 correct answers to this question.

A. Change
B. Realize
C. Preset
D. Run
E. Deploy

Explanation:

The Q-system is used in the following system lifecycle phases:

Change: The Q-system is used to test and validate any changes made to the system before they are moved to the production environment.
Realize: The Q-system is used to configure and test the system according to the customer's requirements and to ensure that the system is working correctly.
Preset: The Q-system is used to test new releases and patches before they are applied to the production system.

In all of these phases, the Q-system serves as a testing and validation environment for changes and new configurations before they are moved to the production environment.

Answer: A, B, C

Question: 68

What are the goals of the Realize phase?
Note: There are 3 correct answers to this question.

A. To adapt the company-specific business processes
B. To test the adapted configuration
C. To perform dry runs of data migration
D. To conduct a fit-to-standard analysis
E. To discover the solution

Explanation:

The goals of the Realize phase in an SAP S/4HANA Cloud implementation project include adapting the company-specific business processes to the standard processes provided by the solution. This involves configuring the system to meet the specific needs of the organization and testing the adapted configuration to ensure that it meets business requirements. Another goal is to perform dry runs of data migration to ensure that the data is migrated correctly before the actual migration is performed.

A fit-to-standard analysis is also conducted in this phase, where the standard processes are compared against the company's specific requirements. Finally, the solution is discovered and any additional gaps or requirements are identified.

Answer: A, B, C

Question: 69

During the change phase, when can a change project be created in the quality system?

A. Only after testing
B. Only when the data is archived
C. Only when the starter system has been deleted
D. Only after the previous change has been imported to the productive system

Explanation:

During the Change phase, a change project can be created in the quality system only after the previous change has been imported to the productive system. This ensures that all changes have been thoroughly tested and approved before being moved into the production environment. It is important to follow this process to avoid any unwanted issues or errors in the productive system.

Answer: D

Question: 70

Which of the following are the priority areas for using the test automation tool for SAP S/4HANA Cloud?
Note: There are 2 correct answers to this question.

A. Regression test
B. Scope and configure
C. End-user acceptance test
D. Fit-to-standard analysis
E. Implementation support for new and changed processes

Explanation:

The priority areas for using the test automation tool for SAP S/4HANA Cloud are regression testing, which involves validating existing processes and ensuring that they continue to work as expected after changes, and implementation support for new and changed processes, which involves testing the new or changed processes before implementing them to ensure that they work correctly.

Answer: A, E

Question: 71

In which of the following steps can you create a value mapping in the SAP S/4HANA migration cockpit?

A. Convert Values
B. Simulate Import
C. Execute Import
D. Validate Data

Explanation:

In the "Convert Values" step of the SAP S/4HANA migration cockpit, you can create a value mapping. Value mapping is used to map the source values of a field to their corresponding target values during data migration. This step allows you to define and maintain the mapping between the source and target values. You can create a value mapping manually, upload it from a file, or use a predefined mapping that SAP provides.

Answer: A

Question: 72

When should you start with the enablement of the end users of SAP S/4HANA Cloud?

A. In the Explore phase
B. In the Discover phase
C. In the Prepare phase
D. In the Deploy phase

Explanation:

End-user enablement should start during the Deploy phase. This phase includes activities such as system configuration, integration testing, data migration, and end-user training. Therefore, it is essential to provide end-user training and enablement during this phase to ensure that users can effectively use the new system after go-live.
This helps to ensure a smooth transition to the new system and minimizes the risk of errors and delays caused by users not being familiar with the new system.

Answer: D

Question: 73

What can enterprises that deploy SAP S/4HANA Cloud in their subsidiaries achieve?

Note: There are 2 correct answers to this question.

A. They can reduce the adoption effort since they can update their system on-demand.
B. They do not need to update their SAP S/4HANA Cloud instance; this is done automatically once The headquarters' system is updated.
C. They can increase their cloud footprint across their enterprise. Correct!
D. They can get firsthand experience of using the latest ERP system from SAP.

Explanation:

By deploying SAP S/4HANA Cloud in their subsidiaries, enterprises can increase their cloud footprint across their enterprise, and get firsthand experience of using the latest ERP system from SAP. They cannot avoid updating their SAP S/4HANA Cloud instance, but they can reduce the adoption effort since they can update their system on demand.

Answer: C, D

Question: 74

What did SAP develop to provide customers with an implementation experience (guided implementation accelerated by tools, templates, and predefined content, clear guidance through each implementation phase, and an agile project management approach) for SAP S/4HANA Cloud?

A. SAP Leonardo
B. SAP Business Objects Project Systems Rapid Mart
C. SAP Activate
D. Accelerated SAP (ASAP)

Explanation:

SAP developed SAP Activate to provide customers with an implementation experience for SAP S/4HANA Cloud. SAP Activate is an implementation methodology that offers clear guidance through each implementation phase, an agile project management approach, and guided implementation accelerated by tools, templates, and predefined content.

It enables organizations to implement SAP solutions quickly and efficiently by providing step-by-step guidance throughout the implementation process. This methodology streamlines implementation and helps organizations achieve their business goals faster while reducing implementation costs and risks.

Answer: C

Question: 75

Which of the following are project phases in SAP Activate?

Note: There are 3 correct answers to this question.

A. Run
B. Ideate
C. Discover
D. Prepare
E. Configure

Explanation:

SAP Activate is a methodology used to guide and manage the implementation of SAP solutions. It is based on industry best practices and agile principles and consists of several phases that help ensure successful project delivery. The phases are:

Discover: In this phase, the project team identifies the business needs and requirements, and defines the scope of the project. This includes conducting workshops and interviews with key stakeholders, and documenting the requirements in a business blueprint.
Prepare: In this phase, the project team prepares for the implementation by creating a project plan, identifying resources, and setting up the project infrastructure. This includes setting up the system landscape, creating a project charter, and developing a communication plan.
Explore: In this phase, the project team explores the capabilities of the SAP solution and determines how it can be configured to meet the business requirements. This includes conducting proof-of-concept activities and creating a solution design.
Realize: In this phase, the project team configures the SAP solution and develops customizations to meet the business requirements. This includes performing unit testing, integration testing, and user acceptance testing.
Deploy: In this phase, the project team deploys the SAP solution to the production environment. This includes preparing the system for go-live, migrating data, and conducting end-user training.
Run: In this phase, the SAP solution is in operation, and the project team provides ongoing support and maintenance. This includes conducting post-implementation reviews and making continuous improvements.

Overall, SAP Activate provides a structured approach to project management and helps to ensure that the SAP solution is implemented successfully, on time, and within budget.

Answer: A, C, D

Question: 76

Which of the following systems is part of a two-system SAP S/4HANA Cloud landscape?
Note: There are 2 correct answers to this question.

A. Quality system (Q)
B. Test system (T)

C. Development system (D)
D. Production system (P)

Explanation:

In a two-system SAP S/4HANA Cloud landscape, there are two systems:

Development system (D): This is where the project team develops and configures the SAP solution. It is used for customization and testing, and is not typically used by end-users.
Production system (P): This is the live system where the SAP solution is used by end-users to perform business processes and transactions.

The Quality system (Q) and Test system (T) are not part of a two-system SAP S/4HANA Cloud landscape. In a three-system landscape, there may be a separate Quality system and Test system used for testing and quality assurance before changes are moved to the Production system.

Answer: A, D

Question: 77

When does the upgrade of the P and Q systems in your SAP S/4HANA Cloud happen?

A. Quarterly, on the first weekend of the quarter
B. On-demand, within one week of your request
C. Once, four weeks after Release to Customer (RTC)
D. According to the wave cycle that SAP assigned to you

Explanation:

The upgrade of the Production (P) and Quality (Q) systems in SAP S/4HANA Cloud happens according to the wave cycle that SAP assigns to each customer. A wave cycle is a predetermined schedule for upgrades based on the geographic region and industry of the customer.

SAP releases upgrades to its cloud systems on a quarterly basis, and each wave cycle is assigned a specific time frame for when the upgrades will be applied to the customer's systems. The exact timing of the upgrades will vary depending on the wave cycle assigned to the customer.

The upgrade process for SAP S/4HANA Cloud is managed by SAP, and customers are typically notified in advance of when their systems will be upgraded. SAP provides customers with access to a preview system where they can test the new functionality and ensure that their existing customizations and integrations will continue to work correctly after the upgrade.

Answer: D

Question: 78

What lays the foundation for the new value levers for SAP S/4HANA Cloud?
Note: There are 3 correct answers to this question.

A. New user paradigms
B. Digital core architecture
C. Technology innovations
D. SAP Cloud Platform
E. Adoption in the LoB

Answer: A, B, C

Explanation:

The new value levers for SAP S/4HANA Cloud are based on several foundational elements, including:

Digital core architecture: SAP S/4HANA Cloud is built on a modern, in-memory database platform that provides real-time analytics and transaction processing. This architecture enables businesses to operate with greater agility and make better decisions based on real-time data.
Technology innovations: SAP is constantly innovating and introducing new technologies that can help businesses optimize their operations and drive growth. Some examples include machine learning, block chain, and the Internet of Things (IoT).
New user paradigms: SAP S/4HANA Cloud provides a modern, intuitive user experience that is designed to be accessible from any device. This helps to improve productivity and user satisfaction.

These foundational elements lay the groundwork for the new value levers in SAP S/4HANA Cloud, which include enhanced business processes, improved decision-making capabilities, and better collaboration across the organization. While SAP Cloud Platform and adoption in the Lines of Business (LoB) are important components of the SAP ecosystem, they are not foundational elements that specifically lay the groundwork for the new value levers in SAP S/4HANA Cloud.

Question: 79

Which of the following end-to-end solutions is part of the Core Finance business priority of SAP S/4HANA Cloud?
Note: There are 3 correct answers to this question.

A. Project Services
B. Inventory Management
C. Accounting and Closing Operations
D. Cost Management and Profitability Analysis
E. Treasury and Financial Risk Management

Explanation:

The Core Finance business priority in SAP S/4HANA Cloud focuses on providing end-to-end solutions for finance-related processes. The following solutions are part of this business priority:

Accounting and Closing Operations: This solution provides capabilities for financial accounting, management accounting, and financial closing operations. It allows organizations to automate financial processes, close their books faster, and gain insights into their financial performance.

Cost Management and Profitability Analysis: This solution provides capabilities for cost accounting, profitability analysis, and activity-based costing. It enables organizations to optimize their costs, identify profitable products and customers, and make informed decisions based on cost and profitability data.

Treasury and Financial Risk Management: This solution provides capabilities for cash management, liquidity planning, and financial risk management. It allows organizations to optimize their cash positions, manage their financial risks, and ensure compliance with regulatory requirements.

Answer: C, D, E

Question: 80

What are some of the benefits of using machine learning procedures in the SAP cash application?
Note: There are 3 correct answers to this question.

  A. Improved overall service quality for Shared Service Centres
  B. Reduced time and effort spent by accountants matching open receivables to incoming payments
  C. Processing of large volumes of incoming payments
  D. Automatic currency conversion based on actual data
  E. Automatic management of petty cash payments

Explanation:

Using machine learning procedures in the SAP Cash Application provides several benefits, including:

- By automating the process of matching open receivables to incoming payments, machine learning can help to improve the overall service quality of Shared Service Centers.
- By automating the matching process, machine learning can significantly reduce the time and effort required by accountants to match open receivables to incoming payments.
- Machine learning can handle large volumes of incoming payments, enabling organizations to process payments more efficiently.

Answer: A, B, C

Question: 81

What are some of the benefits of the Procurement Overview page?
Note: There are 3 correct answers to this question.

A. Increased efficiency of purchasers
B. Supplier network communication
C. Document management
D. Business process acceleration
E. Instant insight to action

Explanation:

The Procurement Overview page in SAP S/4HANA Cloud provides several benefits, including:

- The Procurement Overview page provides purchasers with a comprehensive view of all procurement-related activities, enabling them to quickly and easily monitor and manage their tasks.
- By providing a single, integrated view of procurement-related activities, the Procurement Overview page can help accelerate procurement-related business processes.
- The Procurement Overview page provides instant visibility into procurement-related activities, allowing users to quickly identify issues or opportunities and take appropriate action.

Answer: A, D, E

Question: 82

Which of the following business challenges does the Procurement Overview page address?
Note: There are 3 correct answers to this question.

A. Complex collaboration (internally and with vendors)
B. Complex and time-consuming processes with high volume of purchasing documents
C. Poor end-user adoption
D. Repetitive errors in invoice matching
E. Inconsistencies after clearing of open items

Explanation:

The Procurement Overview page in SAP S/4HANA Cloud addresses several business challenges, including:

- The Procurement Overview page provides a centralized location for all procurement-related activities, enabling better collaboration both internally and with vendors.
- The Procurement Overview page simplifies procurement-related processes, reducing the time and effort required to manage a high volume of purchasing documents.

- The Procurement Overview page provides a user-friendly interface, making it easier for end-users to adopt and use procurement-related processes.

Answer: A, B, C

Question: 83

How is the order to cash process realized?

A. Based on SAP Best Practices
B. By importing the existing processes from traditional SAP ERP systems
C. By refactoring the code used in the procurement and invoice collaboration processes
D. Based on add-ons provided by customers from the retail industry

Explanation:

The order to cash process in SAP S/4HANA cloud is realized based on SAP Best Practices. These are preconfigured business processes and settings that are designed to enable organizations to implement and run SAP S/4HANA Cloud quickly and easily.

The SAP Best Practices provide a comprehensive set of business processes, business scenarios, and test cases that are based on industry best practices and can be customized to meet the specific needs of an organization. By using the SAP Best Practices for order to cash processes, organizations can benefit from preconfigured processes that have been optimized for efficiency and accuracy, as well as from the flexibility to customize the processes as needed.

Answer: A

Question: 84

Which of the following features is new in the Accelerated Customer Returns process in SAP S/4HANA Cloud compared to traditional EPR systems?
Note: There are 3 correct answers to this question.

A. Triggering of each sub-process through separate transactions
B. Automatic booking of materials
C. Flexible compensation for returned materials
D. Automatic generation of the return delivery document from the return sales order
E. Extended Warehouse Management

Explanation:

The Accelerated Customer Returns process in SAP S/4HANA Cloud is a new feature that allows customers to efficiently manage and process customer returns. Compared to traditional ERP systems, it offers several advantages, including:

- When a customer returns a product, the system automatically books the material back into inventory, reducing manual effort and improving accuracy.
- The system allows for flexible compensation options for returned materials, such as issuing a credit memo or replacing the product, giving customers more choices and improving their experience.
- The system automatically generates the return delivery document from the return sales order, reducing manual effort and streamlining the process.

These features improve the efficiency and accuracy of the customer return process, resulting in cost savings and higher customer satisfaction.

Answer: B, C, D

Question: 85

Which of the following roles is required in the end-to-end process for professional services?
Note: There are 3 correct answers to this question.

A. Sales Accountant
B. Resource Manager
C. Billing Clerk
D. Warehouse Clerk
E. Talent Manager

Explanation:

The end-to-end process for professional services involves three key roles: Sales Accountant, Resource Manager, and Billing Clerk.
The Sales Accountant is responsible for negotiating contracts and managing sales orders, while the Resource Manager is responsible for assigning personnel and resources to projects. The Billing Clerk is responsible for creating invoices and managing payment processes.

Together, these three roles ensure that professional service projects are executed efficiently and effectively, from initial sales to final payment.

Answer: A, B, C

Question: 86

In which phase of the project can a project manager create a billing proposal?

A. In the Execution phase
B. In the Fit to Standard Analysis phase
C. In the Contract Preparation phase

D. In the Planning phase

Explanation:

In SAP S/4HANA cloud, a project manager can create a billing proposal during the contract preparation phase of the project. During this phase, the project manager creates a contract with the customer that includes the terms and conditions of the project, the scope of the work to be done, the timeline, and the billing arrangements.

Once the contract is created, the project manager can then create a billing proposal, which is a preliminary invoice that outlines the billing terms for the project. This helps to ensure that the customer understands the costs and can approve them before the project work begins.

Answer: C

Question: 87

What can companies achieve by using demand-driven manufacturing in SAP S/4HANA Cloud?
Note: There are 3 correct answers to this question.

A. They can evaluate forecasts correctly.
B. They can permanently optimize the process flow.
C. They can produce only for real demand.
D. They can work event-driven and empower teams to make local decisions.
E. They can plan for variations along the supply chain.

Explanation:

Demand-driven manufacturing in SAP S/4HANA cloud enables companies to produce only for real demand and work event-driven, empowering teams to make local decisions. This approach helps to permanently optimize the process flow and allows for variations along the supply chain to be planned for.
By using real-time demand signals and data, companies can evaluate forecasts more accurately and adjust their production accordingly. Overall, demand-driven manufacturing provides greater agility, flexibility, and efficiency in the production process.

Answer: B, C, D

Question: 88

What are some of the business benefits of demand-driven manufacturing in SAP S/4HANA Cloud?
Note: There are 3 correct answers to this question.

A. Adapting via feedback based on real time data analytics

B. Achieving an improved and smooth material flow with fewer exceptions

C. Gaining responsiveness to react on real customer demand

D. Maintaining a strong buffer level at each tier to cover safety stock

E. Enabling you to make the right assumptions

Explanation:

Demand-driven manufacturing in SAP S/4HANA Cloud allows companies to produce only for real demand instead of relying on forecasts. This approach helps businesses gain the responsiveness to react quickly to real customer demand, adapt to changing market conditions via feedback based on real data analytics, and achieve an improved and smooth material flow with fewer exceptions. It eliminates the need to maintain a strong buffer level at each tier to cover safety stock, which reduces inventory and storage costs.

Additionally, demand-driven manufacturing enables teams to make local decisions and work event-driven, empowering them to respond quickly to changes in customer demand and other factors. This results in a more agile and efficient production process, leading to increased customer satisfaction and profitability.

Answer: A, B, C

Question: 89

Which embedded analytics capabilities are planned for stage 3 of SAP S/4HANA Cloud development?

A. Prediction and machine learning capabilities

B. Overview pages

C. Insight-to-action reports

D. Functions that allow you to extend the data model

Explanation:

Stage 3 of SAP S/4HANA cloud development includes the planned addition of prediction and machine learning capabilities to the embedded analytics. This will allow for more advanced and proactive insights, enabling users to make data-driven decisions and take action based on predicted outcomes.

Answer: A

Question: 90

What do SAP Best Practices for analytics with SAP S/4HANA provide?
Note: There are 3 correct answers to this question.

A. A step-by-step implementation guide

B. Guidance on how to integrate with SAP Cloud Platform

C. Guidance on how to integrate with SAP Analytics Cloud

D. A manual on how to use SAP S/4HANA Cloud as a data warehouse

E. A set of business intelligence UX components

Explanation:

SAP Best Practices for analytics with SAP S/4HANA provide a step-by-step implementation guide for setting up analytics capabilities in the system. The guide includes recommendations on how to integrate with SAP Cloud Platform and SAP Analytics Cloud, which can provide additional analytics functionality beyond what, is available in SAP S/4HANA Cloud.

Answer: A, B, C

Question: 91

Which of the following tasks can you perform using the SAP Smart Business KPIs app?
Note: There are 3 correct answers to this question.

A. Change the visualization of KPIs

B. Report aggregated results in a tile on the SAP Fiori launch pad

C. Drill down into KPIs

D. Run data mining algorithms

E. Drill down into a data model and modify it

Explanation:

The SAP Smart Business KPIs app provides the ability to visualize and monitor Key Performance Indicators (KPIs) in real-time. It allows users to change the visualization of KPIs, report aggregated results in a tile on the SAP Fiori launch pad, and drill down into KPIs to investigate data further. The app is designed for business users and does not provide the ability to run data mining algorithms or modify the data model.

Answer: A, B, C

Question: 92

Which of the following are characteristics of the SAP S/4HANA Cloud extensibility concept?
Note: There are 2 correct answers to this question.

A. The extensibility concept for SAP S/4HANA Cloud ensures cloud-ready lifecycle processes.

B. SAP S/4HANA Cloud extensions are loosely coupled.

C. SAP S/4HANA Cloud offers reduced extensibility capabilities, allowing only simple extensions.

D. SAP S/4HANA extensions are designed only for SAP consultants.

Explanation:

The SAP S/4HANA Cloud extensibility concept offers cloud-ready lifecycle processes, allowing customers to extend their cloud solution to meet their business needs. It supports loosely coupled extensions, which means that extensions are decoupled from the core of the application, reducing the risk of conflicting changes during system updates.

This approach allows customers to modify and enhance the functionality of their system while minimizing the impact on the core application. Therefore, options for more complex extensions are possible while ensuring cloud-ready lifecycle processes. On the other hand, SAP S/4HANA Cloud provides various extensibility capabilities that go beyond simple extensions and can be carried out by customers and partners without relying on SAP consultants.

Answer: A, B

Question: 93

In-app extensibility applications can be used to add custom fields, use custom forms, or use CDS views for analytics. For whom are these in-app extensibility applications designed?

A. For SAP Your Answer
B. For IT experts
C. For key users (business experts)
D. For consultants

Explanation:

In-app extensibility applications are designed for key users or business experts who have knowledge of the business processes and requirements of their organization. These key users can use in-app extensibility tools such as custom fields and logic, custom CDS views, and custom business objects to extend the standard functionality of SAP S/4HANA Cloud and adapt the system to meet their specific business requirements without requiring extensive IT knowledge or the involvement of external consultants. This allows organizations to tailor the system to their unique needs and stay agile in a rapidly changing business environment.

Answer: C

Question: 94

Which of the following statements regarding SAP S/4HANA Cloud APIs is true?

A. SAP S/4HANA Cloud APIs can be used to connect only SAP systems.
B. Customers cannot use SAP S/4HANA Cloud APIs to integrate SAP systems with their own systems.
C. SAP S/4HANA Cloud APIs can be used to connect only third-party cloud systems.

D. SAP S/4HANA Cloud APIs use SAP Cloud Platform Integration and/or SAP HANA cloud connector to connect to on-premise and cloud systems.

Explanation:

"SAP S/4HANA Cloud APIs use SAP Cloud Platform Integration and/or SAP HANA cloud connector to connect to on-premise and cloud systems." SAP S/4HANA Cloud APIs can be used to connect with both SAP and non-SAP systems, including third-party cloud systems. To connect with on-premise systems, SAP Cloud Platform Integration and SAP HANA cloud connector are used.

Answer: D

Question: 95

Which of the following are characteristics of public APIs used to connect SAP S/4HANA with third-party systems?
Note: There are 3 correct answers to this question.

  A. They can use SAP Cloud Platform Integration.
  B. They use Odata, REST, or SOAP protocols.
  C. They are publicly released on the SAP API Hub.
  D. Each public API can be used for only one operation.
  E. They can only be used to connect SAP cloud systems to SAP on-premise systems.

Explanation:

Public APIs are released on the SAP API Hub and are designed to allow third-party systems to connect to SAP S/4HANA Cloud. They use Odata, REST, or SOAP protocols to enable data exchange and functionality access between SAP S/4HANA and other systems.

These public APIs can be used with SAP Cloud Platform Integration to integrate SAP S/4HANA cloud with other cloud or on-premise systems. Each public API can be used for multiple operations, providing flexibility in integration scenarios.

Answer: A, B, C

Question: 96

Which of the following are capabilities of master data management in SAP S/4HANA Cloud?
Note: There are 3 correct answers to this question.

  A. Mass processing
  B. Master data consolidation
  C. Master data prediction
  D. Master data remediation

E. Master data modelling

Explanation:

Master data management in SAP S/4HANA cloud refers to the processes and tools used to ensure that an organization's critical business data is consistent, accurate, and up-to-date. It involves creating and maintaining a single, trusted source of master data, which can be shared across the enterprise to support various business processes.

Some of the key capabilities of master data management in SAP S/4HANA cloud are as follows:

Master data consolidation: This involves consolidating duplicate or conflicting data from different sources into a single, reliable source of truth. SAP S/4HANA Cloud offers tools such as data quality management, data enrichment, and data harmonization to support this process.
Mass processing: This refers to the ability to process large volumes of master data quickly and efficiently. SAP S/4HANA Cloud provides tools for batch processing, mass updates, and data migration to support this capability.
Master data remediation: This involves identifying and resolving issues with master data, such as missing or incomplete data, incorrect data values, or data that does not conform to business rules. SAP S/4HANA Cloud provides tools for data cleansing, validation, and enrichment to support this capability.

Answer: A, B, D

Question: 97

What are some of the benefits of using master data remediation functions in SAP S/4HANA cloud? Note: There are 2 correct answers to this question.

A. You can change data "en masse" to adapt erroneous master data and ease the correction process.
B. You can easily analyze payment advices and goods movements.
C. You can ensure that product master data complies with the rules for data correctness and completeness.
D. You can use the provided data mining capabilities.

Explanation:

Master data remediation in SAP S/4HANA Cloud provides benefits such as the ability to make mass changes to adapt erroneous master data, thereby simplifying the correction process. This function also ensures that the product master data complies with the rules for data correctness and completeness. By using the master data remediation functions, businesses can save time and effort on manual data correction tasks and improve the accuracy of their data. This can lead to better decision-making and improved business outcomes.

Answer: A, C

Question: 98

What is the purpose of the Discover phase?

A. To test the solution
B. To support the Go-Live of the solution
C. To help customers understand the breadth, depth, and functionality of SAP S/4HANA Cloud, and the benefits it can bring to their business
D. To help customers understand the configuration options in detail

Explanation:

The Discover phase of SAP S/4HANA Cloud implementation is focused on helping customers understand the functionality, benefits, and potential business value of the solution. During this phase, the implementation team works closely with the customer to gain a detailed understanding of their business processes and requirements and identify any potential challenges or obstacles that may need to be addressed. This phase involves a series of workshops, presentations, and discussions aimed at educating the customer about the capabilities of SAP S/4HANA Cloud and its potential impact on their business.

Answer: C

Question: 99

What is the main activity of the Explore phase?

A. Scope and configure
B. Discovery access
C. Fit-to-standard analysis
D. Realize

Explanation:

The main activity of the Explore phase in the SAP Activate methodology is to conduct a fit-to-standard analysis. During this phase, the project team and the customer work together to identify and evaluate the business processes that will be implemented in the SAP S/4HANA Cloud system. The objective is to find out how the standard features and functions of the SAP S/4HANA Cloud align with the customer's business requirements.

The team will document any gaps between the standard functionality and the customer's requirements and determine whether these gaps can be resolved by configuring the system or whether additional development is necessary. The fit-to-standard analysis is a crucial step in the project as it lays the foundation for the subsequent phases of the project.

Answer: C

Question: 100

What is the aim of the Prepare phase?

A. To migrate, integrate, extend, and test your solution
B. To onboard your users to SAP S/4HANA Cloud
C. To configure your SAP S/4HANA Cloud starter system
D. To perform the initial planning and preparation for your deployment project

Explanation:

The aim of the Prepare phase in SAP S/4HANA cloud implementation is to perform the initial planning and preparation for the deployment project. During this phase, the project team defines the project goals, scope, timeline, and resources needed.
They also identify any potential risks and develop a mitigation plan. Additionally, the team prepares for the project kick-off meeting, identifies the key stakeholders, and establishes the communication plan. The outcome of the Prepare phase is a detailed project plan, including the deployment strategy and the timeline for the subsequent project phases.

Answer: D

Question: 101

What does guided configuration for SAP S/4HANA cloud provide?

A. Maintenance master data for SAP S/4HANA Finance cloud
B. Guidelines for the programming of extensions in the cloud
C. Machine learning capabilities for auto configurations in SAP S/4HANA cloud
D. An assisted way to adapt SAP Best Practices for SAP S/4HANA cloud

Explanation:

Guided Configuration for SAP S/4HANA Cloud provides an assisted way to adapt SAP Best Practices for SAP S/4HANA Cloud. It guides customers through the configuration process for their system by presenting a series of questions and options based on SAP Best Practices, helping customers easily and quickly set up their system according to their business needs.

The guided configuration approach reduces the complexity of the configuration process and allows customers to use the system faster, with less effort, and with fewer errors.

Answer: D

Question: 102

Which of the following configurations are performed during the Preset phase?
Note: There are 3 correct answers to this question.

A. Define the transaction types.
B. Define the currencies.
C. Define the organizational structure.
D. Define the chart of accounts.
E. Define the payment block reasons.

Explanation:

During the Preset phase, certain configurations are performed to set up the basic structure of the SAP S/4HANA cloud system. These configurations include defining the organizational structure, defining the chart of accounts, and defining the currencies used in the system.

The organizational structure is defined to determine the different levels of responsibility and hierarchy within the company, and the chart of accounts is defined to determine how financial transactions are recorded and reported. The currencies are defined to determine the currencies used for transactions in the system.

Answer: B, C, D

Question: 103

How can you change the default testing values for a process step when using the test automation tool for SAP S/4HANA Cloud?

A. By using a self-service customizing (SSC) UI
B. By importing the values from another test plan
C. By adding a variant
D. By creating a new test plan

Explanation:

When using the test automation tool for SAP S/4HANA cloud, you can change the default testing values for a process step by adding a variant. A variant is a predefined set of values that you can use to change the default input values for a process step.

By adding a variant, you can customize the test data for a process step and ensure that the testing values match your specific testing requirements. This can help you to conduct more accurate and effective testing of your SAP S/4HANA Cloud solution.

Answer: C

Question: 104

How are the relevant migration objects for your implementation of SAP S/4HANA cloud determined?

A. Manually, by selecting them in the SAP S/4HANA migration cockpit
B. By your account manager based on your request
C. Automatically by the SAP S/4HANA migration cockpit, depending on the activated scope items
D. Based on the licensing agreement

Explanation:

The relevant migration objects for an implementation of SAP S/4HANA Cloud are determined automatically by the SAP S/4HANA migration cockpit. This is dependent on the activated scope items in the system.

The SAP S/4HANA migration cockpit is a tool that supports the data migration process to SAP S/4HANA. It provides a central point of access for all data migration activities, including selecting and preparing data for migration, monitoring the progress of data migration activities, and performing cutover activities.

The scope items are preconfigured business scenarios that define the functional areas of the system that need to be activated to achieve the desired business processes. The migration objects are the data objects that need to be migrated to the new system, such as master data and transactional data.

Answer: C

Question: 105

What is a Learning Journey?

A. A how-to guide for process tutorials in the My Learning app
B. A guided tour embedded in SAP S/4HANA Cloud
C. A document that describes your experience during the on boarding process to SAP S/4HANA Cloud
D. A role-based collection of learning assets for a specific topic

Explanation:

A Learning Journey is a role-based collection of learning assets for a specific topic, such as Finance or Procurement, designed to guide a user through the learning process in a structured and efficient way. It includes various learning assets such as videos, interactive simulations, guided exercises, and assessments.

A Learning Journey can be accessed through the SAP Learning Hub, which provides a personalized learning experience for users. The aim of a Learning Journey is to help users acquire the skills and knowledge they need to effectively use SAP solutions in their roles.

Answer: D

Question: 106

Which of the following applications are embedded in SAP S/4HANA Cloud?
Note: There are 3 correct answers to this question.

A. SAP Learning Hub
B. Migration app
C. Configuration apps
D. Test app
E. SAP Best Practices Explorer

Explanation:

SAP S/4HANA cloud is an intelligent, integrated ERP system that can be used to manage different business processes such as finance, sales, procurement, manufacturing, and more. To ensure that customers can use the system efficiently, SAP S/4HANA cloud offers a variety of embedded applications that are integrated with the core system.
Here are some examples of embedded applications in SAP S/4HANA cloud:

Migration app: The migration app enables customers to migrate their data to SAP S/4HANA cloud. The app includes migration objects that are required to migrate data for various business processes, such as financials, logistics, and others.
Configuration apps: Configuration apps are designed to help customers configure their SAP S/4HANA cloud system. The apps provide step-by-step guidance on how to configure various settings in the system, such as organizational structure, chart of accounts, currencies, and more.
Test app: The test app is a tool that allows customers to test their business processes in SAP S/4HANA cloud. The app enables customers to create test plans, execute tests, and monitor the results of the tests.

Answer: B, C, D

Question: 107

When should you start with the enablement of the key users of SAP S/4HANA Cloud?

A. In the Realize phase
B. In the Run phase
C. In the Prepare phase
D. In the Deploy phase

Explanation:

In the SAP Activate methodology, the enablement of key users of SAP S/4HANA Cloud should start in the Prepare phase. This phase involves planning and preparation activities, such as determining the project scope, identifying the project team, and defining the project goals and objectives.

During this phase, it is also essential to identify key users and provide them with the necessary training and knowledge transfer to perform their roles effectively in the upcoming project phases. By enabling key users in the Prepare phase, they can contribute to the project's success by providing valuable input and feedback on business processes and requirements, which can help ensure that the SAP S/4HANA Cloud solution meets the organization's needs.

Answer: C

Question: 108

At what stage are we in the adoption lifecycle of SaaS ERP?

   A. Acceptance/Enthusiasm
   B. Confidence
   C. Euphoria
   D. Confusion/Frustration

Explanation:

SaaS ERP has been in the market for over a decade now and has gone through several of these stages. Initially, it was in the innovator stage, where a few tech-savvy organizations adopted the technology.

As more organizations became aware of the potential benefits of SaaS ERP, it moved to the Early Adopters stage. However, during this stage, there was still some confusion regarding the technology's implementation and functionality. As the technology matured, it moved to the early majority stage, where more organizations began to adopt SaaS ERP as a viable solution. The technology had proven its value, and the benefits had become more widely recognized.

Currently, SaaS ERP is in the acceptance/enthusiasm stage, where organizations have gained confidence in the technology, and it has become widely accepted. The benefits of SaaS ERP, including flexibility, scalability, and cost-effectiveness, have become well-known and widely recognized. As a result, more organizations are investing in SaaS ERP, and there is a lot of enthusiasm about the technology's potential to transform business operations.

Answer: A

Question: 109

What do S/4HANA Cloud and S/4HANA on-premise have in common?

A. They run on the same upgrade schedule
B. The adoption of new innovations provided by SAP requires a similar amount of time and efforts
C. They share the same scope
D. They are built from one single code line

Explanation:

S/4HANA Cloud and S/4HANA on-premise are both enterprise resource planning (ERP) software solutions offered by SAP. While they have some differences in terms of deployment and maintenance, they are both built from the same single code line. This means that the functionality and features of S/4HANA Cloud and S/4HANA on-premise are fundamentally the same.

They have the same data model, business processes, and user interface. This makes it easier for customers to switch between the two solutions, depending on their business needs.
Upgrades to both solutions are managed by SAP; they may have different timelines depending on the specific version and deployment.

The adoption of new innovations provided by SAP may require different levels of time and effort for cloud and on-premise solutions, depending on the specific deployment and customer needs.
The scope of S/4HANA Cloud and S/4HANA on-premise can also differ depending on the specific deployment and customer needs.

Answer: D

Question: 110

Why does a two-tier ERP approach increase the complexity of the supporting IT architecture?

A. Because processes that are specific to one subsidiary must be replicated in all subsidiaries
B. Because headquarters must backup all subsidiaries ERP systems
C. Because master data management and configuration needs must be harmonized across systems
D. Because integration becomes more complex in multi-vendor setup

Explanation:

A two-tier ERP approach involves having one central ERP system for the parent company and separate ERP systems for each subsidiary. This approach increases the complexity of the supporting IT architecture because master data management and configuration needs must be harmonized across systems. Master data refers to the fundamental data that is used across an organization, such as customer data, product data, and financial data.

If the master data is not consistent across all ERP systems, it can result in data inconsistencies, data duplication, and errors. This can negatively impact business processes, decision-making, and reporting. Therefore, it is critical to ensure that master data is synchronized and harmonized across all ERP systems. This can be a complex task, especially when dealing with multiple ERP systems from different vendors.

Answer: C

Question: 111

Which of the following scenarios covers end-to-end processes between headquarters and subsidiaries in a SAP S/4HANA Cloud two-tier landscape?
Note: There are 3 correct answers to this question

A. Core Finance
B. Recruiting
C. Manufacturing
D. Procure to Pay

Explanation:

In a SAP S/4HANA Cloud two-tier landscape, there are typically several end-to-end processes between headquarters and subsidiaries, including Core Finance, Manufacturing, and Procure to Pay.

Core Finance covers financial accounting, management accounting, and treasury management. In a two-tier ERP approach, the parent company may use a central ERP system for Core Finance processes, while subsidiaries use their own ERP systems.

Manufacturing includes processes related to production planning, material management, and quality management. In a two-tier ERP approach, the central ERP system may manage high-level production planning and materials management, while subsidiaries manage their own detailed production planning and execution.

Procure to Pay covers the procurement process from requisition to payment. In a two-tier ERP approach, the central ERP system may manage procurement for high-level purchasing, while subsidiaries manage their own detailed purchasing processes.

Answer: A, C, D

Question: 112

Which of the following are milestones of SAP S/4HANA deployment with SAP activate?
Note: There are 2 correct answers to this question.

A. Scope items Assessment
B. Go-Live
C. Trial System Subscription

D. Starter System Deployment

E. Contract

Answer: B, E

Explanation:

SAP Activate is a methodology for SAP S/4HANA implementation that uses agile principles and best practices to streamline and accelerate the project lifecycle. The following are the SAP Activate milestones:

Prepare: This milestone involves creating the project plan, assembling the project team, and defining the project scope.

Discover: In this milestone, the customer's current business processes are analyzed, and the functional and technical requirements are identified.

Explore: This milestone includes the creation of a prototype, proof of concept, and testing of the SAP S/4HANA system.

Realize: The Realize milestone is the main implementation phase, where the SAP S/4HANA system is configured and customized according to the customer's requirements.

Deploy: In this milestone, the system is moved to the production environment, and the end-users are trained on the new system.

Go-Live: This is the final and most critical milestone of the project, where the new SAP S/4HANA system is put into production and replaces the old system.

Run: The Run milestone is the post-implementation phase, where the SAP S/4HANA system is monitored and supported.

Contract: This milestone marks the beginning of the project, where the customer signs a contract with SAP for the implementation of the SAP S/4HANA system.

The SAP Activate methodology is designed to be flexible and adaptable to each project's unique requirements, allowing for a faster and more efficient implementation of SAP S/4HANA.

Made in the USA
Monee, IL
22 May 2023